He made the wide oceans and the deep seas.

He made rolling waves and splashing spray.

5

God made dry land –
the high hills and the tall mountains,

6

Heather Henning and Alison Atkins

God Made a World

Lots of little flaps for little fingers!

In the beginning darkness was everywhere.

God said, 'Let there be light!'
And so light shone into the darkness.

Now there was day and night.

God made the air and the sky –

an enormous sky, with fluffy clouds.

the deep valleys and the wide plains.
God saw it and he was pleased
with the land he had made.

7

'Now let grasses, trees and plants of every kind grow on the earth,' said God.

There were tall trees, small trees, bushes and fruit trees; redwood, maple, cherry and oak; apple, banana, pear and pine.

There were climbing plants
and prickly plants,
and waving grasses,
ripe with corn.

There were flowers everywhere.
Red, yellow, orange, purple, pink and blue,
they scented the air.

I wave
my trumpet.

10

Lilies, lavender, daisies, roses and honeysuckle.
God was pleased with all the growing things he had made.

11

God filled the sky with magnificent things –
the yellow blazing sun for daytime;
and the silvery moon at night.

He gave the comets fiery tails.

He made millions of twinkling stars
to shine in the darkness of space.
And God was pleased with what he had made.

13

'Let there be living things in the water,' said God.
So he made shoals of fishes
to swim in his vast oceans:

big fishes, little fishes, round fishes, flat fishes,
so many flapping tails and waving fins!

14

He made teeny-tiny sea-creatures
and great big sea-monsters.
And God was pleased
with the swimming things
he had made.

15

'Let there be living things in the air,' said God.
So he filled the air
with millions of birds and insects.

16

They had wings
that go whirr, buzz and hum.
Birds with feathers
bright as the morning sun,

and butterflies and busy bees
flew through the heavens.
And God was pleased
with the flying things he had made.

'Let there be living things on the earth,'
said God.
So God made lots of animals – all different.

Animals that were furry, smooth, stripy, spotted,
wild or friendly, God made them all.
Soon they were running, jumping, galloping and hopping,

18

slithering, bouncing, climbing and leaping
all over God's world.
And God was pleased with the animals he had made.

Last of all, God made people.
'Let there be people!' said God.
And God made the first man and called him Adam;
and he made the first woman and called her Eve.

He made them to be his friends,
and he asked them to look after his world.
God was very, very pleased with everything he had made.

God loved the world he had made
and he loved everything in it.
And after that, God rested.

Published in the UK by The Bible Reading Fellowship
First Floor, Elsfield Hall, 15-17 Elsfield Way, Oxford OX2 8FG
ISBN 1 84101 352 8

First edition 2003

Copyright © 2003 AD Publishing Services Ltd

1 Churchgates, The Wilderness, Berkhamsted, Herts HP4 2UB
Text copyright © 2003 Heather Henning
Illustrations copyright © 2003 Alison Atkins
Editorial Director Annette Reynolds
Art Director Gerald Rogers
Production John Laister

British Library Cataloguing in Publication Data.
A catalogue record for this book is available from
the British Library.

Printed and bound in China